www.notsocommoncourtesy.com

www.notsocommoncourtesy.com

mitzi taylor

Not So Common Courtesy:
The Owner's Manual

www.notsocommoncourtesy.com

Copyright © 2009, Mitzi Taylor. All rights reserved. This book, or parts thereof, may not be reproduced in any form or by any means without permission from the publisher (me ☺).

ISBN: 978-1-44-210114-2

Special thanks to:

- Taylor Raber and my friends at Qonverge for the cover design. They rock! (www.qonverge.com)
- Ramona my publicist. Brave soul to put up with my moods, crying and photo fright! (ramona@notsocommoncourtesy.com).
- Holly Alway, owner Eidetic Imaging. For making me look good! www.eideticimaging.com

Editing by Mandy L. DeWilde.

Printed and bound in the United States of America.

Contact information:

Mitzi Taylor
www.notsocommoncourtesy.com
mitzi@notsocommoncourtesy.com
800.577.4293

Not So Common Courtesy: The Owner's Manual

---

www.notsocommoncourtesy.com

www.notsocommoncourtesy.com

Pay It Forward Pages:

Use these pages to sign your book before you pass it along. Who knows? Maybe you will get it back after it has traveled around the globe!

Name	**State/Country**	**Date**

www.notsocommoncourtesy.com

Pay It Forward Pages:

Name   **State/Country**   **Date**

Not So Common Courtesy Reader Tips:

www.notsocommoncourtesy.com

Manners are of more importance than laws... Manners are what vex or soothe, corrupt or purify, exalt or debase, barbarize or refine us, by a constant, steady, uniform, insensible operation, like that of the air we breathe in.

Edmund Burke

www.notsocommoncourtesy.com

Thank you to:

- My friend, Sue, for continuing to tell me I was funny and should write a book.

- All of my friends who contributed stories: Modacious (Tom), AnnMarie, Julie, Dawn, Suzie, Rachel, Chadly and Butch.

- Of course, my mom, Shoey and my dad, Big Baby, who set such a wonderful example.

- Janelle, who motivated me by telling me she would quit if I didn't finish the $^%$ book (and she NEVER swears!).

- My honeydew for always being positive with me, even when I didn't deserve it.

- Ramona for telling me what to do after I finished writing the book.

- And finally YOU. Yes, all of the discourteous people out there that motivated me to write this book. Without you to give me all of the examples in this book, I would not be where I am today — having sold 3 books!

---

www.notsocommoncourtesy.com

www.notsocommoncourtesy.com

The Journey

Introduction

My Motivation

Past & Present

Uncommon Courtesies:

- Drive-Thru's
- Communication
- Personal
- Public Places
- Traveling
- Driving
- Pets

Final Thoughts

Bonus: Pass-It-Along-Pages

Resources

---

www.notsocommoncourtesy.com

www.notsocommoncourtesy.com

Introduction

Picture this:

You are shopping at the local supermarket and you have to use the restroom. There are five stalls, two of which are so disgusting you wonder if they have EVER been cleaned. You find one acceptable and do your business. You head to the sink to wash your hands. When you step away from the sink you realize you have been leaning in a pool of water on the countertop and now it looks like you wet yourself and you have to go back out in public. Wonderful. Now what?! Well, that is what this book is here to address. We should not be looking at "now what"; we should be looking at "why was the water there in the first place?"

When is the last time you went an entire day without thinking about the lack of Common Courtesy in our society? A month, a week, every day? It may seem to be a small thing, but even with the example above (which, of course, just happened to me) Common Courtesy would have required that the person(s) who slopped water all of the counter would have cleaned it up. She made the mess; she should be accountable to clean it up. Am I right or am I right?

Just by listening to people talk, I have an idea that the general public feels the way I do; Common Courtesy is not so common these days and it sure isn't getting any better. When you have time, jump online and read the articles and blogs regarding the lack of Common Courtesy in our society. Hmm...if we all think people are pretty darn rude, and Common Courtesy is lacking, and we all seem to want it back, then I wonder who is responsible for bringing it back? Of course "not *me*" we seem to be thinking because, you know, we are also a society that lacks personal accountability. So it *must* be someone else's problem/fault.

During the last year I have noticed an increase in the amount of comments from friends, neighbors, and even strangers on the street regarding a general and increasing rudeness, selfishness and a lack of respect. No, not directed at me, directed more pointedly at you, Q Public. People not holding doors for others, no "thank you's," "I'm sorry's," and don't even get me started on the lack of customer service. It got me thinking: what happened to Common Courtesy? Is it dead, dying a slow and painful death, being held hostage? I really didn't know and neither did anyone I polled, at least not with any certainty. Though, I did get lots of opinions on where people think it has gone. So, I decided to go searching for Common Courtesy because I really do miss the good old days when people made eye contact and said "hi" when you passed, when clerks said "thank you" after you handed over your hard earned money and when people would let you in when a lane is unexpectedly closing. You know – that thing we used to call *Common* Courtesy. This book is about my journey, findings, and about my hope for the future.

Now, I already know your first question: why should I read it? Well, I'll tell you. Because you need it. And if YOU don't, someone you know does and you should pass it along. We all need it. How else are we going to revive Common Courtesy – which I found out (I don't want to ruin the ending or anything, but) is near death. WE have to do something – this is **your** chance to save the world! Or at least a small part of it anyway. Without Common Courtesy what would our world be like? I'm guessing you have a glimpse of it already but let me create a more vivid picture. Read on…

Yesterday my friend Tom was waiting in an express lane at the local grocery store. Even though this is a fairly common occurrence, I want to describe his experience, which again, is not out of the ordinary. Bear with me; you will see yourself somewhere in this story:

Like most people in our society, Tom is always in a hurry. He wants things when he wants them and trusts that the systems our commercial/retail world has set up for us — the consumers — should help meet his needs, FAST (express lanes, drive-thru's, etc.). Out of five express lanes available at the store, only one is open to all of the 15 people wanting to check out quickly, hence, of course, the reason for the EXPRESS LANE's existence.

First of all, Tom reports that there are at least four people who have far over the **stated** ten items. So, he can only deduce that we have a literacy (and serious math) problem in our community. Of course, they are counting their ten loaves of bread as one, 17 cans of soup as two and so on. There are two women in line who are on their cell phones, yakking away, not paying attention when the line moves forward. The guy behind him has a kid that is playing in the candy on the knee-leveled display. So far, he has burrowed in next to Tom's shins 15 times, barging back out each time with a different candy, knocking into Tom while asking,

"Dad, can I have this one?" The dad has said no 15 times. The kid starts to throw a fit. What the dad has failed to say is, "No you may not have any candy and if you ask one more time we are leaving the store and you will not be allowed to come back with me next time."

A clerk decides to open the lane adjacent to the lane Tom is standing in. Finally! Tom has only moved **one** person in **five** minutes (before you accuse Tom of being too impatient, remember, he is in the *express* lane). The clerk stands behind the register and yells, "Next please," without making eye contact with anyone. You know exactly what happened. The LAST person in line runs over and gets FIRST in line at the newly opened lane. It sure takes a nice, patient minded individual to do that. Keep in mind, the two ladies are still yakking on their cell phones, the kid is still asking for candy, and Tom is getting really irritated. He sighs loudly to the cashier when it is finally his turn to check out, tells her that she really should have the NEXT person in line go first, blah blah blah, proceeds to take it out on the cashier, acts all impatient and stomps away after paying for his purchases. Who did he think he was kidding? He looked like the ass in that scenario not the rude guy who cut in front of everyone.

As he was telling me this story which, by the way, I have edited for language, I started really thinking about the lack of Common Courtesy and personal accountability in our society and what I could do about it. This is just one simple example of a huge problem.

I reflected on Tom's story. I wanted to count all of the instances of Common Courtesy missed. Can you name them all? For those of us who have not seen Common Courtesy in awhile, let me help you out:

#1. First of all, the store should have associates who are **trained** to work in the express lane, meaning they understand the concept that people use the express lane because they want out quickly.

#2. The store should allow the clerks to hold people accountable to follow the guidelines. If someone has more than ten items they should be sent to a normal lane. Yes, I know, as soon as a clerk tries to send someone to a different lane the **customer** gets all loud and difficult, like they aren't the one that KNEW it was an express lane, that THEY didn't really ignore the sign that says "ten items or less". Of course, this is never you. You never act that way because you possess Common Courtesy.

#3. Now, for the two women on their cell phones. Really, what is so important that you have to talk to people on your cell phone while you are checking out in the express lane? What cannot wait until you are outside or at home? I know people get bored. Perfect time to use this great technology, but there should be some things sacred, like not holding everyone else up because you cannot do two things at once – slide your debit card thru the reader to pay for your groceries while chatting on your phone about how awful your bathing suit shopping experience was. If everyone were focused on "express," the express lane would serve its purpose once again. I will address cell phones in more detail later.

#4. What is up with the parent who lets his/her child run wild, bumping into others, not caring that he or she is being completely disrespectful? We will also address parents later.

#5. Then there is the clerk who opened her lane and yells "Next!" Here we go with training again...clerks should be taught to walk up to the next person actually *in* line, look them in the eye, walk them over to the isle and let them be next. This would be great Common Courtesy and, by the way, excellent customer service.

#6. As a customer, you should have your method of payment out and ready when it is your turn to check out. Don't waste your time - and everyone else's time in line behind you - digging through your wallet looking for payment. You knew when you got in line that you were you going to have to pay for your items.

Yes, Common Courtesy has fled our society. Why should we care? "We don't have time for Common Courtesy anymore!" people exclaim. Look around you. Pay attention to how people treat each other. Do we really want to continue down the road we are traveling with Rude and Selfish? My crystal ball tells me we won't like where we end up in 10 years...scrap that, NOW! If everyone who reads this book would accept the personal responsibility of being respectful to one another and living your lives with

Common Courtesy, a small part of the world would be a better place to be. Are you buying into this? Great. Now, let's move on and figure out how to do it!

My Motivation

Experience: Here is another example. I was waiting in line at a movie rental place and the person behind me dropped some change on the floor. I bent down and crawled around to help pick it up as her 3 kids, who apparently were not trained to help in situations like this, just watched. I scooped up the 5 pennies that I could see, and turned around to hand them to the woman. She snatched them out of my hand like I was going to keep them, opened her purse, dropped them in, and gave me the evil eye. No "thank you", no "please can I have my hard earned $.05 back", nothing. Just the evil eye. Ok lady, $.05 was really going to put me into the millionaire category. I was stunned. People, get a grip!

The whole reason I sat down to write this book is to help our society get back to a place where we are respectful of one another, kind to one another, and we can all just get along! A place where we can walk in someone else's shoes before jumping to conclusions. A place where we think of others before ourselves…

I know, you're thinking, what a load of CRAP! Maybe, maybe not. What is one person really going to do? HELLO

— the Pink Ribbon started with one person taking a stand! I really do think I have a point here. If you have EVER had the thought about someone, "what an *&!#%, didn't their parents ever teach them Common Courtesy?!" this is a book for you, more importantly for *them*. It should make you laugh, it will make you think, it probably will make you mad, and I know it will make you want to go out and buy this book for anyone who you deem does not have the decency to possess Common Courtesy! (My blatant attempt at selling more books? Or someone trying to change the world one person at a time? You decide).

I would actually love it if you disagree with anything I have written. At least it has made you think, which is more than I can say for the five people you just bought this book for (remember, who don't have Common Courtesy?). Have fun, give me feedback, and whatever you do, have the Common Courtesy to not be reading this book when you should be doing something else!

Past
& Present

Let's start our journey. There was a time in the recent past that the phrase *Common Courtesy* was used to explain behaviors that everyone was expected to know and practice. Some of the more common, Common Courtesies were:

- Do unto others as you would have them do unto you.
- Think before speaking.
- RSVP – please reply as soon as possible.
- Hold doors open for people.
- Give up seats to those that need them.
- Send "Thank You" notes.
- Cover your mouth when coughing/sneezing.
- Children should address elders as Mr., Mrs., Miss, Ma'am or Sir.
- Say "please", "thank you" and "you're welcome".
- Say "hi" as you pass someone and look them in the eye.

This used to be the way people conducted their lives. There was a personal accountability to being courteous. Your manners and etiquette were not just about how you treated others, it was a show of your attitude in general.

Common Courtesy, like common sense, does not require any level of education or status. Anyone and everyone can participate. But we need to remember we are not like cats with their kitty litter boxes, we are not born with this knowledge, we must be taught by someone.

We would say it is common sense to not leave a candle burning when you leave your house. We would also say it is Common Courtesy to say "Please" and "Thank you." Again, common *anything* is not so common! Just ask your local fire department how many house fires are caused by candles left burning. Let's stick with Common Courtesy.

Courtesy – commonly defined as: the gesture of goodwill without the expectation of something in return; marked by respect for and consideration of others; a courteous, respectful, or considerate act or expression (that sounds great! I want some of that!). Many words can describe what we are talking about: manners, proper behavior, being polite, decency, kindness, respect for others, thoughtfulness and consideration for others.

I have to admit, I do understand some of the reasons people are not courteous to others. Here are some of the reasons that I hear people use:

- Lack of time. People are trying to pack so much into so little time, they feel they don't have time to hold a door for someone because they have to get milk that of course they are sure is almost sold out and there are people that are going to beat them to the last bottle so they HAVE to hurry…I am sure someone is picking up the last bottle right now…hurry, don't hold that door for the next person. As a matter of fact, close the door in his or her face quickly to slow him or her down!

- A rush to be selfish can overcome Common Courtesy tendencies (i.e. Wal-Mart & Black Friday). This situation involved not only a lack of courtesy, goodwill, respect, and personal ethics, but hopefully prosecution for some people who choose the wrong path. If we learn nothing about how to treat each other and to stop being so selfish from this example where the Wal-Mart employee, Jdimytai Damour, was trampled to DEATH on Black Friday in 2008 by bargain hunters, we deserve what we get. Absolutely unforgivable. When did saving a couple of dollars override our sense of what is right and wrong?

- No one else is doing it. Okay, so the clerk is rude to you and you know you are going to make it so much better by one-upping him and being even more rude — that will teach him! I'm not going to be courteous if you're not! I even heard a parent say, "What, teach my kid courtesy so he can be laughed at in school and have everyone call him a sissy-boy because he is holding the door for people? NO WAY!" Apparently, two wrongs do make a right.

- It's not cool to be nice. Unfortunately the media is not portraying Common Courtesy as the "in thing". Being rude and discourteous is apparently more fun and cool. This brings up a major difference in how different generations seem to be interpreting Common Courtesy. I do believe it is okay to adapt the Common Courtesy Owner's Manual to fit all new generations. I do not believe it is okay to not have a Common Courtesy Owner's Manual at all. This reminds me of the saying, "What is right is not always popular; what is popular is not always right" (Thomas Jefferson).

- I know there are more excuses, but I cannot think of them right now. I am a bit distracted by someone in this coffee shop where I am sitting here quietly working on this book. I am quite positive he NEEDS this book. I wanted to print it out and give him a copy, but I didn't bring my printer with me, because THIS IS NOT MY HOME OFFICE! This guy is sitting at a table next to me, talking SO loudly on his cell phone that no one in a mile radius can hear themselves think. I can only assume he thinks he is alone in his own house because he has removed his shoes and is moving his feet around rapidly to air them out – which by the way, smell. He is in a very public place and severely lacking Common Courtesy. He isn't thinking that some of the people here come to the coffee shop for some semi-quiet time, to reflect on the world and ourselves…not to listen to his spiel on insurance and why everyone needs more of it. GEEZ!

So the Journey begins. We have looked at what Common Courtesy is and the fact that it is not common. Now we need to focus on specific areas where Common Courtesy is dying and figure out what we can do about it.

We are in this together. Have fun, take notes, take notes in the book, talk about it with others, and please email me areas that I might have overlooked:

mitzi@notsocommoncourtesy.com

Thank you. ☺

Life is short, but there is always time for courtesy.

Ralph Waldo Emerson

Drive-Thru's

At the Bank

When at the bank drive-thru, who of you has ever been so angry that you literally wanted to jam your foot on the gas to ram the car in front of you as hard as you can to move it out your way, because that person has five complicated transactions and 10 minutes later you are still sitting in the same spot? Or when someone gets up to the window and THEN starts filling out whatever paperwork they need to turn in? Or how about when the person in front of you goes through the *drive-thru* to argue something on their statement?! Do they realize how inconsiderate all these situations are? Probably not, so this is for them:

1. *How many transactions are you limited to at the drive-thru?*
   Two. As in one deposit into savings and one deposit into checking. Or cashing one check and withdrawing cash. I was looking through an old bank-teller's training manual and found a definition of a bank drive-thru transaction:

   "…we offer the drive-thru experience (love that, "experience") to our busy customers as a way for them to bank conveniently in the most efficient way possible…"

Translation: We want in-and-out service. I almost don't want to have to stop because I want it so quickly.

Learning points for repeat offenders: Maybe the banks should be providing an Orientation to their new customers explaining what most of the real world already understands (about the two transactions at the drive-thru, etc.). I think we should also add this to the Parenting Manual. When your kids are old enough to use the drive-thru experience, teach them the mostly unwritten courtesy rules exposed in this book. Thank you in advance.

2. *What should you have ready prior to driving up to the space-station-like-canister-thing?*
ANYTHING and EVERYTHING you might need. Please have your slip filled out, signed, any ID you might need, and any bank cards. You are not **allowed** in line until you have everything filled out. And no, this does not mean that you block the lane so no one else can

get in. Please park in the parking lot and when you are ready, then slowly, cautiously move into the next available lane.

3. *How long should you sit in front of the space-station-like-canister-thing after your transaction has been completed?*

   ZERO seconds. MOVE! This is not the time to make a journal entry into your register, or the time to file away paperwork, or to get on your cell phone, or finish your cigarette so you can throw it out the window so everyone in the 3 cars behind you can smell the lovely odor of your butt. Just move ahead so the person behind you can use the drive-thru. Check your statement and count your money in the parking lot, out of the way of others. If something is missing or wrong, you can always go into the bank. This way, you aren't holding up the line and wasting everyone else's valuable time.

4. *What do smoking cigarettes and cell phones have to do with drive-thru's?*

   NOTHING! May you hit the concrete barriers with

your side view mirrors the next time you are too busy with your cigarette or cell phone to bother making your transaction in a timely manner. This makes you not worthy to use the drive-thru and we all know it.

5. *What transactions are allowed in the drive-thru?*
   Anything that can be turned around FAST by the bank employees. No, this is not the route to go when you have $150 in change and you want dollar bills, or you want to argue something on your statement that is 3 months old. Please remember the "two transaction" rule.

6. *When at the ATM:*
   All rules above apply to the ATM machine. Also: If it is a walkup machine — give the person some breathing space please. It really is not going to go any faster just because you are standing as close as you can get to the person using the machine. This is one of those times "You know you are standing too close…when" the person in front of you keeps turning their head and looking at you with suspicious eye contact that is saying "I think you are reading my pin number and I don't

want you to do that so please step back a few paces!" Again, thank you in advance for our breathing room.

Fast Food

Hey, whether we admit it or not, most of us eat fast food from time to time. Here's the thing, like with bank drive-thru's, "Fast Food" says it all. We want the food fast and we want it now. I have beefs with both the consumers and the establishments on this one.

General Public/Consumers

If you know you are going to place an order, which of course you do as soon as you pull into the lot, please have your cash ready or at least in a handy and retrievable spot. I cannot tell you how much exercise my eyes get when I engage in Olympic eye rolling as the person in front of me gets all the way to the "Pay Here" window and THEN starts digging around the car for loose change to pay for his or her meal. I've seen people actually get out of their car at this point to check the back seat for money while of course talking on the cell phone making sure to update the person on the other end about the quest for change. "No way! I just found $0.35 in the trunk under the spare tire…bonus!" I have also been behind a Suburban filled with people who order, get to the "Pay Here" window, and then ask for each order to be announced separately so each person can pay, SEPARATELY. This is the equivalent of going into the building and waiting behind 7 people to order (just to spell it out, defeats the FAST FOOD drive-thru philosophy). If I am behind one car, no matter how big it is, I expect to have to wait the length of time for maybe 2 meals – not 7! Do you NOW see why I needed to write this book?! (Now, I just want you to know, for research purposes, I sacrificed and gained 10 lbs for this section. A percentage of the proceeds from this book will be going toward a gym membership. Thank you).

How many orders should you place in a drive-thru?

Let me put it this way: how many orders from one single car would YOU want to wait behind at the drive-thru (correct answer is two maximum). Yes, there is a difference between having seven people in one car with seven orders and having seven cars in line at the drive-thru each with one order. At least the average consumer can count the number of cars waiting, assume they will all have 1-2 orders per car and decide if they want to wait. When one of those cars waiting place seven orders, it screws up the entire Fast Food system. Everything comes to a screeching halt. This is typically when you hear the drive-thru speaker start to say, "whaa whaa, whaa, whaa, whaa, whaa…" See? Broken.

How do you make sure you have the correct order?

Fast food establishments over the years have invested many thousands of dollars in systems to be able to get Total Order Accuracy (repeating your order after you place your order, video screens that show your order, repeating your order while looking at the receipt *and* in the bag before they hand you your order, etc.). They still can't seem to get it right. I don't expect it anymore. I kind of think of it as Mystery Meal Surprise. If you are not into the Mystery Meal, no problem. You have every right to check your order before pulling away from the drive-thru. But please PULL AHEAD to do that. Once you are out of the way of other drive-thru customers, you can calmly sit in your car checking for "no mayo", counting your fries, making sure you got your two packs of salt, your diet pop, and your 1…2…3…10 catsups, then carefully put everything back in the bag and slowly pull away. Still want to stay at the window while checking your whole order? No problem. After everyone in the world reads this book (my goal), they are all going to do that TO YOU to see how you like it.

Ooops, NO NO NO – the point is to start being more courteous to each other…I know I should be all about "treat other people the way you wish to be treated" and all that stuff. NOT UNTIL EVERYONE ELSE STARTS ACTING THAT WAY TOWARD ME! Yeah, that's right. Do unto others as you are done to… (This was an example of how easy it is to fall into the trap of killing Common Courtesy. Let me reset…).

Okay, better now.

Parents and Drive-Thru's:

I get the whole "got to give kids choices so they grow up to be responsible people" thing. But this is not the time to allow your kids the freedom of choice. Be aware, one day I might ram your car when I am behind you and I hear you ask your 5 year-old, "honey, what do you want?" and I hear your 5 year-old say, "I want grilled cheese." You say, "Oh honey, they don't have grilled cheese here, they have…" You then list off the entire menu while going back and forth with your child for five minutes deciding "are you sure you don't want fries, remember last time you ate all mine..." Please, for the sake of everyone behind you, get the kids the chicken nuggets and call it good! It's just lunch, right? Keep the compromising for the dinner table at home. Consider this, if you offer them too many choices it may turn into a $20,000 therapeutic opportunity when they grow up and find they can't make ANY decisions.

The Post Office

I am working on this section of the book at holiday time. A wonderful time to find Common Courtesy alive and well on our planet, or so I thought.

Okay, wake up! I found a glitch. While waiting at the drive-thru mail station at the post office, my friend and business manager Janelle just found a bit of an issue with Common Courtesy. Her story, told while very red in the face:

> "I am sure you will agree that the time to put stamps on all of your holiday cards (all 107 of them) is when you have pulled up to the drive-up box during the holiday season. Absolutely! No one will be waiting behind you. This person of course, couldn't have *planned* to put the stamps on earlier so they could just DROP the envelopes in the box and DRIVE on. No. That would mean they were being courteous and thinking that there might be about, oh I don't know, like maybe 1000 other people needing to drop their cards in the box…"

She went on, but for censor's sake, I will leave it at that. A good lesson for all, don't you think? Plan, prepare, drop and move on.

Tipping

Even though this does not have to do with drive-thru's, we were talking about food, so let's talk about tipping. Tipping is not something you *have* to do. For the most part, it is our choice if we tip or not. Common Courtesy appears to be between 15-20% depending on the service. I personally believe in tipping and typically tip well. I also expect service to be extraordinary and deserving of a tip. Yes, you can make your point when you have lousy service by leaving a penny, but would it not be more respectful of you to let the waiter know that you were not happy with the service? This is, of course, after you have received your food. Be nice to your wait staff. I have a firm belief that everyone should be forced to work in a job waiting on people (cashier, waitress/waiter, etc.) so we can all appreciate how grueling it can be.

End of Chapter Challenge:

1. **Don't make the above mistakes.** The drive-thru systems in place work really well when we follow the sometimes unwritten rules of these systems.

2. Teach your children the rules.

3. Be patient with people who forget the rules, or imagine that maybe someone didn't teach them the rules. How are people supposed to know if no one tells them?

Today, give a stranger one of your smiles. It might be the only sunshine he sees all day.

Quoted in P.S. I Love You, compiled by H. Jackson Brown, Jr.

Communication Courtesy

Do you know anyone who doesn't say "goodbye" when ending his or her telephone conversation with you? All of a sudden you are talking along, and no one is there. Or you just hear the dial tone when you ask a question. What is that?! Is there a fear of separation here? Is it that he or she is in such a rush to get to the next thing that he or she can't even say goodbye? Please, if you are one of these people, email me and tell me why you don't say goodbye after a phone conversation! Let's look at a few other areas surrounding the art of communication where Common Courtesy is not so common…

"Please" and "Thank You"

How often in a day do you hear these words? Not sure? I challenge you to stop reading at this point and take a day to tally up the count. Also be paying attention to how many instances where it would have been appropriate had the rules of Common Courtesy been used. Ok, stop reading now, but please begin again after your count.

Insert Count: _____

A Gentle Reminder on When to Use "Please":

Try uttering this word before you ask someone to tell you if you have something horrendous stuck in your teeth; "Will you hold please?" (on the telephone vs. "Hold please" and then you are sent into Hold Hell where no one gets back to you – also, always wait for a response); and of course when you ask a friend to do anything! "Pass the salt, please" or "Please pick up that wonderful new book on Common Courtesy on your way home today…"

A Gentle Reminder on When to Use "Thank You": Certainly when you receive your change from the

gas station attendant; when someone holds the door at work open for you; when someone tells you "Your hair looks great today!" (vs. "Ohmygosh, I'm sure squirrels nested in my hair last night and I have not been able to do a thing with it today!"); and when the Money God (a.k.a. the ATM) gives you your money (the people who watch those surveillance videos might appreciate it!); and so on.

Make your own lists:

When you should say "Please".

1.

2.

3.

4.

5.

6.

7.

8.

9.

10.

When you should say "Thank you".

1.

2.

3.

4.

5.

6.

7.

8.

9.

10.

RSVP's

The acronym RSVP comes from the French expression *répondez s'il vous plaît*, meaning "please respond". Okay, you didn't necessarily need to know that, but what you do need to know is this: This acronym is still widely used here is the United States. Typically you will see this on invitations to showers, parties, weddings, etc. I believe we Americans have taken RSVP to mean: please totally ignore that fact that the host/hostess needs to know a head count for meals, seating, plan for potential conflicts when inviting certain people, etc. I think most people use it this way: RSVP - **R**esponding **S**eems **V**ery **P**ointless.

I don't give many parties. If asked, one reason would be that I sometimes have a low tolerance for people and if you get a group of people together, you will find lots of examples of the absence of Common Courtesy. So, I simply choose to abstain, which led me to interview the husband of my good friend Sue. Francis is a very organized person. He firmly believes in some of the 'old fashioned' Common Courtesy standards like RSVP'ing. He was more than happy to tell me about his wedding and how the whole RSVP thing went.

"RSVP'ing is ridiculous! What a waste of ink to put it on an invitation. I was taught that if you wrote "RSVP" on an invite, it meant that people needed to respond. Period. They would RSVP to let you know they would be attending or would not be able to attend. This system should work beautifully. I knew I needed a definite head count for the dinner so the caterers could plan the food and the hall could put out enough chairs and tables to accommodate all those who said they would be attending. I needed the response by the date specified on the invitation in order to meet the deadline set by the caterers and the hall. Reality was different than my imagined perfect system. I had people respond that they were going to attend and then didn't show up. Nice waste of my money there at $18 a plate for dinner. I had people not respond at all and then show up. Nice seating arranging we had to do at the last minute. I had people respond "2 people" and then they brought their three children. I thought I had put "Adult Only Reception" on the invite, but maybe it only printed clearly on my sample…"

Immediate Personal Action Plan:

Please RSVP. It is as simple as saying "Yes" or "No". You do not need to go into a lot of detail if you don't want to. Use the S.A.S.E. (self addressed stamped envelope - yes, another acronym) that most people put in the invite. Or email them, for pity's sake, how easy is that?! Whichever the way, just be sure to do it. There will come a day when you need people to RSVP and they won't or don't. Then you'll be the angry one at having your plans screwed up.

Cell Phones

I read the most perfect sign at a restaurant yesterday. "Please do not get in line until you are off of your cell phone." YEAH! For those of you who think you can do two things at once, like decide six inch or foot long, what flavor bread, meat, toppings and condiments, warm or cold, AND be talking to your husband about the plumbing bill while there are 10 people standing behind you all in a hurry to get their food, think again! Have I ever done it? Sure, and I loathe people like me. I could write a whole book just on cell phone etiquette. But I won't. Not today anyway. But I do want to go over some foundational cell phone guidelines:

1. Understand that everyone can hear you. My friend, Dawn, was waiting for an appointment in her doctor's office and there was a gentleman talking on his phone about his commitment issues with his girlfriend. Dawn admitted his conversation was more interesting than the Golf Digest magazine that she was pretending to read (she doesn't golf). Dawn's

story: "He looks over and catches me listening and gives me a dirty look. Okay buddy, there are no rules about being an idiot, choosing to talk in a totally public place about very private things. If you choose to subject everyone within listening distance to the intricacies of your conversation, all bets are off!" Yes, I say, go Dawn!

2. Why is it when someone gets on a cell phone, they assume they have to scream for the other person to hear them? I have to tell you, cell phone technology is such that we do not have to speak any louder than we would on any other type of phone device. Really, they will hear you. Oh, except maybe if you are talking on your cell phone somewhere where you should not be talking on your phone like A MOVIE THEATRE!

3. Here is an easy one, but amazingly enough, one people do not follow: Turn your phone off in places you should have your phone off, like: movie theatres, museums, libraries, children's

plays, conferences, training sessions, funeral homes, graduations, restaurants, etc. And please, don't get mad when someone (with an attitude or not) reminds you to turn it off. The glory days of the early 1990's, when people thought you were cool when they found out you had a cell phone, are gone. It's not a rarity anymore, so there's no need to show it off.

4. Be aware, most people in our society, even if they have a cell phone, are annoyed by people talking on their cell phones in public places. Examples:

→ One man I was talking to suggested we ban cell phones from public places just like we banned smoking. Hmmm.

→ Another woman, we'll call her "Joan," was in the restroom at an airport. There was a gal in the next stall talking to a customer on her cell phone. Joan was so annoyed that she proceeded to continuously flush her toilet, and then she went out to wash her hands and turned all of the blow dryers on at once. Rude you think? That's what Joan thought! Joan's point was, if that customer only knew where business was being conducted! Joan thought she should let him/her know!

→ A woman was recently in front of my mother at the grocery store with a huge load of groceries in her cart. The woman was on her cell phone. The line was moving forward but the woman was so engrossed in her call that she was not. My mother, who is very patient and nice, finally asked the woman in a friendly tone to move forward and start putting her stuff on the belt, "or if you are not ready to check out, I can go ahead of you". The woman got offended, gave my sweet mom a really dirty look, let the person on the other end of the line know how rude she was being treated, and huffed and puffed putting all her stuff on the belt one item at a time (as she was one handed, the cell phone occupying her other hand of course). The woman proceeded to talk on her phone through the coupon phase, the "That is supposed to be on sale" phase and the pay phase, "How much?! Are you sure?" Then when she had been given her receipt (which is a universal sign of "move on!") she continued to stand at the end of the line, put her receipt away still talking on her phone, closed up her purse, still talking on her phone, and then finally just stood there in the way of the credit card reader, still talking on her phone. My mom had had it at this point. She pushed her cart into the woman's ankles and gave her an "Oh I'm so sorry, I didn't realize you were still there...five minutes after you checked out!" Sometimes, and I think we all have to agree, we will have to gently remind people that they are severely lacking in courtesy (see Pass it Along pages in the back of the book).

5. This is a good one for all of us to abide by. My friend, Chad, met one of his friends, Bill, at a local coffee shop recently. They had not seen each other in awhile and Chad was looking

forward to catching up. Right from the get-go, Bill kept taking calls from his cell phone. "Oh, I have to take this call," Bill would say. Or "This is a guy I have to talk to." This continued to the point that every time Chad would start a sentence, Bill's phone would ring and he would take the call. Chad got the impression they were not all work related calls when Bill mentioned a few times his escapades from the night before. It didn't take Chad long to get the hint. So he picked up his own cell phone and dialed Bill. Bill had to end a call to pick up Chad's call. Bill answered his phone. Chad calmly said, "Hi, this is Chad, who is sitting right across the table from you. If you would like to schedule another time to catch up, have your people call my people." Chad hung up and walked out of the coffee shop.

Lesson: always keep in mind who and what is important to you. Treat them (or it) accordingly. No one likes to feel second rate to a phone call.

Email

Why do we think when it comes to cyberspace that all Common Courtesies go out the window? Misspelled words, ALL CAPITAL LETTERS, too many people in the cc box... Please do not think you are cool and use abbreviations or text language with people you *know* will not know what you are talking about. People like me. For example, the abbreviation: BM. I thought BM was "I need a bathroom, I have a BM brewing." No, apparently it's "bite me." Did you know there are many levels of BF (best friend)? There is BFF (best friends forever), BFFL (best friends for life), and BFFLNMW (best friends for life no matter what). I am not sure what would drive a BFFL to a BFFLNMW. Not sure I want to find out. How about IMHO? You figure this one out.

Also, it would be nice if you signed your emails. You may think we know who cooljock@abc.com is, but you would be mistaken. May I offer you some more email tips:

- Use spell check, *please*!

- Fill in the "subject" line. We all get so many junk emails that if the subject line is not catchy and pertinent, most of us will delete it. So much better to have a "Please come to my book signing party!" than to put "Book Info".

- Don't be tempted to forward chain-letters. Those superstitious "You will have really bad luck: your dog will die, your roof will fall in, your car won't start and no one will like you anymore unless you send this to 52 people" emails, jokes that really aren't funny, or the ones that could get your "friends" in trouble if you use their work address that are really clogging our inboxes and taking precious time we don't have to weed out and delete. Thank you.

- Bcc: would be to deal with the person you are having conflict with, not "Blind Carbon Copy" his or her boss to stir up trouble.

- Finally, believe it or not, but email is NOT a conflict management tool. When you receive a snarky email from someone, what do you do? Delete? Or do you "Reply" and then sharpen your nails on the keyboard by being just as snarky - if not snarkier - back then hit "Send"? Honestly, is that going to help or hurt your relationship with that person? If you had just picked up the phone and asked "What's up with the snarky email?" you may have found out quickly that there was no intention of the tone. Someone was just in a hurry to get you information.

Immediate Personal Action Plan:

Google "email etiquette" and follow the rules, please. The world will thank you and become a better place.

"Thank You" Notes/Letters

It used to be that when someone bought you a gift, you would send them a kind note expressing how much you appreciate and love the thought, effort, etc. I loved those days! Shoot, these days I will accept a "Thank You" email. Yes this practice is time consuming, and, yes, this practice seems to be going by the wayside. Do we really want it to? Isn't it nice to receive a note that the person received the gift, liked the gift (even if he or she auctioned it back off on eBay) and appreciated your effort/thought? I think it is. I bet you think so too.

End of Chapter Challenge:

1. Even though communication is becoming more and more informal, please pay attention to who you are communicating with. The goal of communication is to have Message Sent = Message Received. Sounds easier than it really is. Tailor your message to your receiver. How would they like to receive your message? How will they best hear you?

2. Please make a legitimate effort to use more cell phone etiquette. The world will thank you and so will my mother, who might just be that lady behind you at the grocery store (so watch your ankles!).

Don't wait for people to be friendly, show them how.

Author Unknown

Personal Courtesy

Punctuality

Suzie, a good friend of mine, talks about a family member of hers that has his "Jeffrey Standard Time". This means 20 minutes later than everyone else is going to be there. They hold up dinner for Jeffrey, opening gifts, lose reservations…all due to the fact Jeffrey can't seem to get there on time. She complains about it all the time. I finally asked her, "Why does everyone wait for Jeffrey? Why don't you stop enabling him and follow your original schedule?" "Oh, we couldn't do that" she said, "That would be rude!" Who is the one not being courteous? Jeffrey. Ok, so how would you handle this one? You don't want to do onto others – meaning because he is being rude, you just say "screw you, snooze you lose!" But, on the other hand, we can't enable people to continue their discourteousness or they won't learn. Besides, why should we, the courteous people who are on time, have to suffer at the expense of the tardy person?

Learning Points:

- Please, be on time.

- Call if you are going to be late.

- Do not feel put out if people started without you.

- Be on time next time - it's that simple.

If you punctual people have a good enough reason to wait, then you may certainly hold up your activity until the tardy party arrives. If not, please commence the activity and do not make all of the people that were there on time wait for one missing person or family.

Waiting

We all have to do it and we **all** hate it. So…

- Plan ahead. If you are going to the Secretary of State office, bring something to read. At least you can sit and wait these days. And don't forget to take a number, or you'll really be sorry.

- Remember, no cutting in line. Everyone's time is valuable, not just yours.

- Sighing, eye-rolling, looking at your watch or any other action displaying your annoyance doesn't make the people ahead of you go any faster.

- When at a restaurant, if the hostess told you it will be a 30 minute wait, please refrain from approaching her station every five minutes and asking how much longer it will be. He or she does know how to do his or her job. If she says 30 minutes, it will most likely be 30 minutes.

- If you own a company where people have to wait for service, a product, etc., be like the Disney Company.

People hate to wait in line at an amusement park, so Disney came up with the "Fast Pass." Not only does this eliminate more people waiting in line, but they are spending more money with all of their extra time. Ingenious!

- In the waiting room, please be aware you are in a public place and behave accordingly.

Respect

- What/who deserves respect? Age? Knowledge? Being famous? Do famous people deserve more respect than a homeless person we pass on the street? If you answered "yes", spend some time reading about Mother Teresa, Gandhi, or others who lived the theory: we are not alone in this world. Everyone deserves respect (except those who choose not to embrace this concept of course).

- Agree to disagree. Respect the opinions and decisions of others, even if you disagree with them. Sure you can argue your point, but remember to check yourself and what you are saying to prevent looking like a complete hothead.

Cleaning Up After Yourself

I really do have an issue with trash. You will notice in many of the chapters I manage to throw in some tips on how everyone should be picking up their own trash.

Amazingly, I am still surprised when I encounter a situation where someone does not clean up after themselves. Take your local coffee shop. Joe Public goes to the counter buys a Grande Latte and Danish, proceeds to take his (*his*) purchase to the closest table, enjoys his goodies, gets up to leave, and then leaves his empty cup, Danish wrapper and napkin on the table. Um…thought that that was *his* stuff once he paid for it, which would mean that *he* should take care of his trash. Apparently, not so.

Next time you visit a coffee shop, fast food establishment, the movies, etc… look around to see if people are cleaning up after themselves. Are you? Remember: If everyone cleaned up after themselves, the world would be a much cleaner place.

End of Chapter Challenge:

1. Try to do one nice, unselfish thing everyday. Put money in someone's expired meter, pick up a discarded cup from someone's parking lot and throw it away, let the poor soul who is trying to merge into your lane get in when everyone else is not letting him safely do so. Email me your list monthly (this will hold you accountable!).

Courtesy is as much a mark of a gentleman as courage.

Theodore Roosevelt

Public Places

Doors

Perhaps I should stoop to the level of some by opening the door just wide enough for me to enter and letting it slam shut in someone else's face, stand on the other side of the door and do the "na na na na na" thing. How hard is it to hold the door open for someone who is about 30 seconds behind you? Not very. You should hold the door for:

- Someone loaded down with stuff
- People needing assistance with the door (i.e. a mother with a baby, someone on crutches, someone with many packages, etc.)
- Children
- And anyone who is only a few paces behind you

I held the door for a man and his apparent five children the other day. One of the kids walked through first. I continued to hold the door. Then three more children went through. Finally, the man holding the last child went through. Yes, I was still holding the door. Four out of the five kids were at least 10 years old. None of them looked at me or said anything to me, they just walked on by. Now, according to the notes from above, one or all of them should have said "Thank you" to me and taken my place to hold the door for the rest of their family. I really don't mind being the doorwoman. That is not the point. Not So Common Courtesy is about each and every person thinking about it and trying to live it. A "Thank you" changes everything.

Personal Space

This is a great one. Did you ever see that Seinfeld episode where they talked about the "Close Talker" and how annoying it is to have a conversation with someone standing about one inch from your face? We can all relate to this because we each have our own sense of personal space. Now, do we pay taxes on our personal space? Of course not, so this means that we don't really own it. But we all know where our personal space boundaries are. It may be different for each of us, but as soon as someone trespasses, we immediately react. Let's look at some examples of how I am tying into personal space. I think you will enjoy it.

Picture standing in a line (anywhere). You are relatively happy, with few worries. The world is at peace. Then you sense someone entering into the line behind you. Suddenly, your high alert alarms are going off. In your internal rear view mirror, you notice that this person has moved into your personal space. The alarms in your head are so loud that you whip around to look at this intruder; ready to kill if necessary (some really are that passionate about their personal space). You find an unsuspecting victim not paying any attention to you, but who is invading your territory. You try to take a step forward, but alas, he moves with you! You shuffle to the left, sure enough, he shuffles too! You give him a dirty look. He's oblivious. You send warning signals: dirty looks, loud "hmph's," and "awhumm's," but the invader is still in your space. You're not quite sure how to ask him to move back, due to the non-ownership issue, so you put up with it and release a major sigh of relief when at last the intruder moves on. Your space is safe once again. One thing to be aware of, other cultures view personal space very differently! It is not right or wrong, it's just different.

So how would Common Courtesy handle this? Well, by getting over it. Don't we have bigger issues to worry about and think about? Do you really think they are trying to invade your personal space to take it over? To conquer it? Or you could politely ask the person to take a few steps back for whatever reason you need it (to breathe, so your (silent) alarms stop going off, etc.). Yes, it is uncomfortable, but it is usually only temporary.

Elevators

Do's:

- Understand that the people inside the elevator have the right of way. Wait until they have all exited safely before barging in. Leave them room to exit.

- Please hold the elevator when you see people running toward it.

- Know what floor you are going to prior to getting on the elevator.

- Make room for others.

- Make eye contact and say hello to others.

Don'ts:

- Push and shove while exiting the elevator. People will make room if you politely ask them to.

- Talk on your cell. You are in a claustrophobically small steel box, possibly with others. Make friends, not enemies.

- Continuously push the "Door Close" button. Think Green. It will be a better use of energy if the elevator fills up for the trip than for you to have a personal elevator all by yourself.

Moving Walkways/Escalators

It is okay to just stand on a moving walkway. Just make sure you are all the way over to the right. Please take your stuff with you. Obviously, when your stuff is in the way, people who need to keep walking to get to where they need to be, can't. Enjoy your rest and know your stuff is safely with you.

Garbage & Cigarette Butts

I have always wanted to ask people who throw their trash out in parking lots, out the window, on park grounds, on airplane floors, etc., "On a serious note, who do you think is going to pick that up? How would you feel if I came to your house with a big ole' garbage can full of nasty smelly stuff, dropped it all over your living room, and without a care in the world walked back out the front door?" I do not see the difference in the above examples. Both are awful.

Driver, when you flick your cigarette butt out the window of your car, who do you think is going to pick it up? Do you ever see trash on the side of a highway and say, "What a bunch of slobs in this county, who would just throw their fast food wrappers out of their car while driving along the highway?" Look in the mirror lately? I ran across one guy who I actually had an opportunity to ask why he just threw his butt out the window. His response, "I didn't want it stinking and dirtying up my ashtray in my new car." You have GOT to be kidding. I see this daily and it never fails to upset me. "But it disintegrates" they say. Yeah, in about 40 years. Let's all get together and do something about this.

The next time we are behind someone who throws their cigarette butt out the window, we will: _____

(email me and fill in the blank!).

Pick up after yourself. Understand that we all want to live on a clean planet — do your part. It will make a difference. And, thank you.

Smoking

For the most part, an individual is entitled by law to smoke. Of course, laws are always changing. Areas where smoking is legal are decreasing. When a smoker chooses to smoke in public where it is legal, he or she is affecting others. This is where courtesy comes in. The tobacco industry (www.ncbi.nlm.nih.gov) recommends "Common Courtesy" as:

> "The solution to potential conflicts over smoking in public places and as an alternative to policies that restrict or ban smoking".

Specifically, the industry suggests that nonsmokers "mention annoyances in a pleasant and friendly manner" and that smokers ask others, "Do you mind if I smoke?" (Office on Smoking and Health, Centers for Disease Control). As my nonsmoking friend AnnMarie puts it, "Right. Like I am going to tell a smoker to move or stop because they are more than likely giving me cancer. Have you ever seen a pissed off smoker? They get mean!"

Immediate Personal Action Plan:

- If you smoke, be very aware you are not alone on this planet. The air that you are filling with smoke, is shared air. No one owns it but we all have to do our best to keep it pure for everyone's health. Try not to do it around nonsmokers.

- Please dispose of your butts in an appropriate container. The highway, parking lots, someone's lawn and the cement right in front of the building you are about to walk into would not be considered "appropriate containers".

Movie Theatres

Remember the literacy problem we discussed in the beginning of this wonderful book where we talked about people not being able to read the "10 Items or Less" signs? Well, I think there is a hearing problem as well. You know how in movies they not only state the "No talking, trash in the receptacles, please be courteous to others" stuff on the screen prior to show time, they also say it out loud. And we still don't get it. Have you ever "Shh'd" someone and had them get really angry at *you?* Right, didn't you know you pay $20 to go see a movie in the theatre just so you can hear people having conversations around you? And to give you an even better experience, people feel the need to talk on their cell phones as well. And then there are the people who really seem to struggle with the packaging that snacks come in. You know the packaging that makes more noise than the sound from the movie and the person is totally oblivious to it, crackling along, happy as can be.

- Going to the movies is a wonderful group activity, UNTIL the movie starts. Yes, this includes the previews. Once the previews start, going to the movies becomes a SOLITARY activity. Once the credits start rolling, you may WHISPER.

- Take care of your trash as it is yours to take care of.

- If there are only a few people in the theatre, don't sit right next to them or right in front of them. Not sure if this is common practice or if I am a weirdo magnet. ALWAYS happens that someone will sit one seat away from me when I go to a movie by myself even though there are only 20 people in the whole theatre. Remember the section on Personal Space.

Public Restrooms

I am really thankful for public restrooms. They can sure come in handy. But really, what is worse than a public restroom? The smell, the TP (toilet paper) all over the floor, the lack of TP, water EVERYWHERE, no soap, then if there is and you use it, you have to touch the totally disgusting doorknob on your way out anyway (because of course no one held the door for you), so you defeat the purpose and have to wash your hands all over again. If people treated the public bathroom like it was their own and company was coming over this would be a totally different experience. It is like someone gave people a license to completely forget Common Courtesy when it comes to public bathrooms. Is it really ok to slop water all over the sink, mirror and floor and not care that the next person who uses that area, leans up against the counter to reach the soap dispenser and gets water all over the front of their khaki pants and it looks like they wet themselves? Might seem ok, until it happens to you that is!

I took a very informal poll of my women friends to find out, do they sit on the toilet seat or hover over it when going to the bathroom. Almost all hover. Whichever is your method, please make sure that general area is all cleaned up when you exit the stall. This definitely applies to men. Yes, you have the ability to aim. Aim correctly. If your aim is not so good, no problem. Just please be sure to clean up after yourself.

Steps:

1. Head into an unoccupied stall.

2. Take care of business.

3. Clean up after yourself. Leave the stall as clean as you would if it was your very own stall.

4. If the TP runs out, see if you can find more to put in the stall. We all hate to be put in the situation depicted in the Seinfeld episode *The Stall* where Elaine realizes too late that she has no TP in her stall. She sees shoes under the stall next to her so asks politely if they have any TP to spare. "No," exclaims the woman, "I can't spare a square; there are no squares to spare!" Elaine was SOL (shit out of luck).

5. After soaping up and washing your hands (PLEASE, I beg all of you to wash your hands!) and toweling off, please wipe off the counter and mirror where you splashed water all over the place. I am not saying don't splash. Just clean up your little mess before you walk out. This is our responsibility when we walk into a public restroom (or private for that matter!). The front of my pants thanks you in advance.

Example of Why We Need Common Courtesy!

Awhile back, I was at a kid's holiday party. I had two beautiful, borrowed children with me that wanted to sit with the rest of the kids in front of Santa. There were not enough chairs, so I went and carried one chair over and sat it down. I went back for the second one and found that a parent who had been standing there took the first chair that I had brought over. She saw that I had two children I was trying to seat. She saw me put the chair down and heard me say to the children, "One of you sit there and I will be right back with another chair." I asked her politely to move. She just looked at me and said, "You snooze you lose." A PARENT says this to me in front of all of the kids and other parents. WOW. I could feel Common Courtesy getting weaker and weaker by the second...dying of a mortal wound...

Sneezing/Coughing

In the age of some serious contagious airborne diseases, please COVER UP!

Real generosity is doing something nice for someone who will never find out.

Frank A. Clark

Travel

Airports & Flying

Did you ever watch that reality show that was based on people's airport experiences (A&E Network, 2003)? It didn't last long, but what a hoot! If you travel a lot, you see this stuff live, which is even better. People get so bent out of shape when their sense of control is taken away. You know, the airlines are not out to get *you*. I know it feels like it, but they aren't.

I travel quite a bit. It is not fun to travel these days. I tend to view the airline industry like healthcare – it is going to implode. If you need any encouragement that we are in dire need of some Common Courtesy in our society, travel. It is unbelievable how people seem to leave their brains at home when they decide to get on a plane to go somewhere. Here are some unwritten rules and tips for the masses. Please take note – if we all work together, maybe, just maybe our airplanes will start to leave on time.

- Note to self: you are going to have to go through security. Yes, you will have to take your shoes off, and belt and jacket…so be prepared. Before you get in line, put all of this stuff in your carry-on to save time. If you are wondering what to do while you are waiting in line to go through security, read the wonderful signs they have put along the route to help all of us be better prepared.

- Don't argue: it will get you nowhere, fast. Arguing will most likely get you to the individual security check which takes even more of your precious time. Be cooperative and pleasant. The security staff is trying to make your plane trip safe. Hello, 9/11.

- Wait your turn: especially when they are boarding the plane in sections and your section is last. The plane will not leave without you and no one is going to take your seat.

- Overhead compartments: if you are sitting in the back of the plane, use the overheads that are in your area. I typically try to sit in the front section of the airplane and am amazed when I finally board how all of the overhead bins are full. How can that be? They just started to board my section. Well, it is because all of the #@$%^# in the back of the plane put their stuff in the front, easier to grab on the way out. Did you ever think about the fact that someone sitting up front will have an EXTREMELY difficult time coming all the way back to your section to find overhead space? If you are one of these people, watch what happens on your next flight. Total chaos. Still not buying in to using overhead space near your seat? While you are watching people struggle, also notice how the plane is not taking off on time.

- Smaller carry-on luggage: if you have a carry-on that will fit under the seat in front of you, put it there. The overhead bin space issue is getting very out of hand. I understand why people are bringing more and more carry-on luggage. With the extra luggage fees and the lost luggage game (is my luggage going to make it with me? This should become a new gambling avenue), no one wants to check bags anymore. I get it. But, please use some smarts and Common Courtesy.

- You know you are a self absorbed flier when: Are you one of those people who boards out of section, stands in front of your seat, puts your bag in the overhead bin, takes your coat off, stuffs that in the overhead bin, decides you need something out of your bag that is in the overhead bin, rifles through your bag, deciding that maybe it is in the bag you are going to stuff under the seat in front of you, sits down, then pops back up needing something else from your bag, in the overhead bin. Then, of course you have to push your stewardess bell to get a pillow and blanket — right then. Do you even realize that there are 100 people trying to get seated? Do you even see us sighing at you, glaring at you and trying to telepathically make you disappear? You are also the one who decides to use the restroom after the pilot has asked everyone to be seated for takeoff. Yes, I travel a lot and these people drive me NUTS! There is no better place to see people so oblivious of other people's needs than flying. We are definitely living in a "me" society.

- Armrest rule: the isle gets the outside armrest; the window seat gets the armrest by the window. The poor soul in the in middle should get both of the armrests in the middle. Fair is fair.

- Reclining your seat. Yes, in theory, your seatback is yours to recline. Close your eyes just for a moment. Work with me on this, close your eyes. Remember the last time you flew? The flight attendant had just provided you a full cup (which of course equals about 2 sips – but hey, NOT complaining - at publication pop is still free) of Diet Coke in your cup along with a snack of peanuts and you had a magazine you wanted to read? Okay, so you put down the handy plastic tray that is provided for just this purpose. There. Everything in its place, your hands are free to choose between the pop, peanuts, scratching your head or turning the pages of your magazine. Everything in your world is good. Until WHOOSH...BAM! The guy in front of you decided to recline *his* designated seat. Too bad that you now have your once full cup of pop in your lap, your peanuts have fallen into never-land under your seat and your magazine is all soaked.

Recliners: please take a peek behind you to see if it is ok to recline. There may be a mom with her kid back there, Tony Robbins with 12 foot-long legs, or someone who is using his/her tray and if you recline would cause them to not be able to use it. If okay to recline, do so SLOWLY. There is no rush on this. Really. You only go back about 2 inches. You'll get there. Thank you.

- The Lavatories: on longer flights they are still serving drinks, which involve drink carts that take up the whole aisle. Is this the opportune time to go to the restroom? NO. They *do* announce that they are going to start the beverage service. Go before they start or after they finish.

- Speaking of bathrooms…pretty much everything applies from the earlier segment on public restrooms. Just a note: The Mile High Club has officially disbanded. Get your kicks elsewhere.

- Cellular phones: do you really need to give someone the play-by-play of your travel on your cell phone? "We are pulling away from the gate…we just landed…we have unbuckled our belts and are getting our carry-ons…I am rushing to get off the plane, cutting in front of people because they are not moving quite fast enough out of their seats even though I am not really in a hurry. Blah, blah, blah…" Use your cell phone wisely. Hey, texting works just as well. Please don't do either of these when you are supposed to be de-boarding.

- Flying with children: Okay, traveling with children is about as much fun as having a root canal with no anesthetic. But parents, it is your responsibility to ensure your children get on board, are seated, and remain seated. When you get to your isle is not the time to decide who is going to sit where, having your kids cry and scream, "I want to sit next to the window!" Look behind you, do you see all of the people waiting to get to their seats? Please, think of them by planning ahead and sitting down in a timely fashion.

End of Chapter Challenge:

1. Take your brain with you when you travel.

2. Be very aware that you are not alone on this planet.

Beginning today, treat everyone you meet as if they were going to be dead by midnight. Extend to them all the care, kindness and understanding you can muster, and do it with no thought of any reward. Your life will never be the same again.

Og Mandino

Driving

According to Ford Driving School "the golden rule of driving is to treat other drivers the way you want to be treated. You should obey traffic laws, drive responsibly, and avoid taking unnecessary risks." Great advice! (www.laforddrivingschool.com).

This should actually be an easy chapter. I have actual WRITTEN laws that back me up here. Let's review a few of the courtesies on the road, shall we?

Construction Zones:

You know as well as I do that when there is a sign saying "Lane Closed 1 mile ahead," they aren't kidding. Your lane will be closing. Let me ask you, are you one of those people who stay in the lane that is closing until the last second and then expect to be let in by one of us who moved over when we were supposed to and have been waiting patiently (this is a relative term) in the long line of cars??? If you are, let me ask the question that is on everyone's mind: Who in the HELL do you think you are? Yes, you are busy. Yes, your time is valuable. Are you saying that our time is not? That we, too, are not busy? In the words of a few research subjects who admit to blowing past all of us:

- "Well, you guys are just stupid for waiting."
- "Suckers!"
- "Oh yeah, there is always some poor soul that lets me in."

Yes, this book is teaching us to be more kind to one another, more forgiving, BUT you do not deserve my kindness when you are planning on abusing it! Move over when you are supposed to.

Turn Signals:

When did people stop using their blinkers when making a turn? It may never have been a problem, so it went by unnoticed when we were patient drivers. But now, in the age of "Road Rage", we travel about a foot behind the car in front of us, so when someone does not use his or her blinker, it affects us. And we cuss and swear, and call the driver an idiot and worse things. It couldn't be *our* fault that we had to slam on the brakes to avoid hitting the non-blinker-using @#%^* in front of us because we had road rage and were tailgating. No, it never is. Please, stop being lazy and use your blinker.

Parking Lots:

My friend Sue has the biggest heart of anyone I know. She takes in all of the wounded animals, buys food for the pantries, and never says "No" to those in need. She definitely does not need coaching on Common Courtesy, except for one area. She has a big problem, as well she should, when she is heading for a parking spot, calmly moving toward it with her car and someone whips in ahead of her.

As Sue was telling me about another instance of her Parking Lot Rage that had just occurred, she indicated she was close to a "TAWANDA" moment. If you are note sure what a "TAWANDA" moment is, let me explain. The word comes from the movie *Fried Green Tomatoes* when the main character Evelyn finds someone about to pull out of a good parking space at the Winn Dixie. The man leaving waves to her, showing her he intends to let her have his spot. As she starts to pull in, a red convertible VW Bug with two young sassy girls whips into the space from the opposite direction. When Evelyn says politely to them that she had been waiting for that spot, they say "Tough" and that they are "younger and faster" and walk away laughing. What Evelyn does next I know we all have wanted to do, but don't (and won't). She gets a look on her face, yells "TAWANDA!" and proceeds to continuously ram the Bug until the girls come running back out. "Are you crazy?!" they scream. "Face it girls, I'm older and have more insurance."

Great scene! But it definitely works out better in the movie than it would in real life. This is one of those "don't try this at home" moments.

Lesson to be learned:

It is very obvious when someone is waiting for a certain parking spot. Let them have it. Also, don't fight for parking spaces. In most cases there are plenty of spaces, we are just too lazy to take the ones farthest from the store.

Cell Phones

- At time of publication, according to the Governor's Highway Safety Association (GHSA, www.ghsa.org) talking on your handheld cell phone while driving is illegal in five states (California, Connecticut, New Jersey, New York and Washington). Many more states are also adopting Text Messaging While Driving Bans.

- More ammunition: June 29, 2006, University of Utah psychologists published a study showing that motorists who talk on handheld or hands-free cellular phones are as impaired as drunken drivers (Human Factors: The Journal of the Human Factors and Ergonomics Society).

- According to Virginia Tech/NHTSA (National Highway Traffic Safety Association), the No.1 source of driver inattention is use of a wireless device.

Note to self: where is it still legal to talk on your cell phone while driving, take note: it might not be legal for long.

Take it from someone who has been there: while driving across the state last year, in a hurry of course, I was talking to a brand new potential client on my cell phone. This was our first conversation. I was setting a beautiful stage of how my company could help her with their leadership development. "Oh yes, we customize our programs to fit your needs..." The conversation was going along smashingly. While entering a construction zone (and exceeding the speed limit), all of a sudden I notice a police cruiser off to the side, hidden by trees. "Oh shit!" I exclaim out loud, into the phone, into the ear of my brand new potential client. That was our first and last conversation.

Cell phones and driving do not mix. If we can't even DRIVE while using the cell phone, how are we going to be COURTEOUS?!

Doing Other Things While Driving

Simple. Don't.

Miscellaneous

- Did you know June is Lane Courtesy Month? The National Motorists Association (NMA) has designated June as Lane Courtesy Month and is asking motorists to **"Do the *RIGHT* Thing!"** Lane courtesy "is the simple act of moving to the right to allow faster traffic to pass. This act of courtesy will significantly improve highway safety. By not obstructing other drivers, we are allowing traffic to flow more smoothly. When traffic flows smoothly, there is less tailgating, less weaving in-and-out of traffic, and therefore fewer accidents". (www.motorists.org/lanecourtesy/home/whylanecourtesyisimportant).

- Another tidbit: On the National Motorists Association website (www.motorists.org): "American drivers are renowned for neither understanding nor appreciating the importance of lane courtesy, i.e., slower traffic keep right and faster traffic pass on the left". Do we really want this reputation?

End of Chapter Challenge:

1. Remember how you felt when you forgot to move over and all of a sudden you saw your exit coming up within sight? You tried to move over using your blinker, but no one was letting you in? Then, all of a sudden a car slows down and waves you over so you can catch your exit. Remember how you felt about that person? Like you wished you could both have pulled over so you could give them a hug? Be the wave-over person for someone else today. **Pay it forward.**

No act of kindness, no matter how small, is ever wasted.

Aesop

Pets

I get that not everyone loves pets. I am a dog person. When people come to my house, my 65lb golden retriever, Lucy, is going to give them love and expect love in return. This dog is my kid. When I go to other people's houses, I don't expect them to put their kids in another room and close the door. Please don't expect me to do the same with my dog. Yes, for the most part I prefer my dog to your children. Yes, my dog lives in my house and it is more hers than yours. If you don't like pets, don't come over.

On the other hand, I DO like people to come over and I want to be courteous. So, my suggestion is to find some common ground. When you decide to own a pet, you sign up for the responsibility of owning a pet. Just like Common Courtesy is mostly unwritten, so is pet Common Courtesy.

- Train your pet not to jump and slobber all over people.

- Ask your visitors to refrain from sitting on furniture that the dog/cat lives on, so they don't freak out when they go to leave with 12 lbs of fur on the back of their black pants.

- If you have a barker, get some help (for the dog). That constant noise can drive someone crazy. There are many tools and resources to assist you in training your pooch to be more peaceful.

- Dog obedience classes are a MUST for all dogs. And guess what? You CAN teach an old dog new tricks. In doubt? Catch an episode of *It's Me or the Dog* on the Animal Planet Channel.

- Pick up after your dog. We have a Dog Beach where I live and every year we are in danger of losing it due to the people who don't pick up after their dog. Hey – this was on your responsibility sheet when you signed up for a pet, remember?

- When you have company, please don't let your cats roam around on the counter or kitchen table. Particularly if you have just prepared snacks or dinner for your company. This is a high probability barf-o-rama situation.

End of Chapter Challenge:

1. Admit if you need some help with your dog. If you don't get chosen for the next *Dog Whisperer* show, find a local pet obedience class. Any dog can learn new tricks, or in this case, courtesy.

2. No matter what kind of pet you have, don't expect everyone to love him/her the way you do. Let people choose their comfort zone with your pet. If cats freak your guests out, try to keep your cat from crawling on them.

Courtesies of a small and trivial character are the ones which strike deepest in the grateful and appreciating heart.

Henry Clay

Final Thoughts

Wow. That was a lot to digest, although I know I have not addressed all areas of Common Courtesy. So, now what?! Take a few days and really pay attention to your world. Are you finding the examples in this book in your world? What are you prepared to do about it? I have an idea…..

Be the change you want to see in the world!

Gandhi

Just like you, I am in a bit of quandary about the future of Common Courtesy. Do we need to rewrite the manual for the new age? How long will it be before no one remembers any of the great common courtesies from our past? Will Common Courtesy be something kids study in the ancient textbooks that have dust all over them and they proclaim, "No way – like, can you believe they did THAT?!" Common Courtesy is already like 8 Track tapes. I said to a "kid" (about 18 yrs old) the other day – "You should say 'thank you' when someone holds the door open for you." The "kid" said, "Why in the world would I do that, if they didn't feel like holding the door, they wouldn't." Alright, he had a point. But, I still think I did too.

My hope for the future:

I really hope we get back to a place where Common Courtesy is again *common*. I also think we should be okay with updating courtesies for the new age. For example: My friend Sue recently received an email "Thank You" for a shower gift. In the old days it was proper to send a handwritten card as a sincere "Thank You" for a gift or sentiment. The replacement of the card with email is a great use of technology and time and in my humble opinion should be accepted.

Read on for more ways to make Common Courtesy more common in your life…

Here are 10 ways you can use this book:

1. Use it for research. Sign the front, date it and pass it on to someone. See if it ever comes back to you! How many people's lives were affected by people being more courteous?

2. Go Green! Read it, become courteous and then pass it along to someone else who needs it, hence, recycle it!

3. Be like my friend Julie: a woman in a parking lot was being very discourteous by yelling at Julie that she parked too close to her precious $40,000 house-payment car. As Julie was in between the yellow lines, and had every right to park wherever she wanted (she was pretty sure the discourteous woman didn't own the parking lot at Target), she did park there, then proceeded to tell the woman to "Get a life." What she should have done was after the woman left to go into the store, put this book under her windshield wiper along with a note: "Thank you for helping me find someone that deserves this book!"

4. Use it for a coaster at a dinner party. You will showcase your literary genius AND it can be a conversation starter during awkward pauses. "Oh, I forgot to tell you guys about my experience at Hanna's school! I went in to talk to the teacher about Hanna's latest grade, and the teacher did not even have the courtesy to …"

5. Give a copy to your doctor or your dentist as a thank-you for saving your life. Maybe they will leave it in their waiting room. People in waiting rooms REALLY need to read this!

6. Next time you travel, leave one in the seat pocket in front of you. Two things could happen: a flight attendant will pick it up, read it, and next time help you with your bag that will not fit in YOUR overhead bin because someone in the last seat used your bin; OR the next passenger to sit there will pick it up, read it, and not fight with you for the middle seat armrest which of course is legally YOURS because you got stuck with a middle seat.

7. Next time you are in a coffee shop, sit and read it with the cover facing the person who believes this public area has become their new private office. You know the guy…he has his laptop open, his Bluetooth in his ear, and is talking so loudly that no one can have a conversation around him. And he gives you dirty looks for giving him dirty looks. Maybe when he sees the words "Common Courtesy" in the title, he will get the hint. If he doesn't, hit him upside the head with the book, then throw it down on his table!

8. Fill in this blank: how are YOU using this book? Email me and tell me! _____

9. You know the person who sits by you in your cube farm at work? The one who uses speaker phone and yells? The one that makes you want to crawl out of your skin? Even though the "Not So Common Courtesy @ Work" hasn't come out yet (but is in production), you can leave this book on his or her desk when he or she is out to lunch with a gift card for $20 and a note: "Be the first to pick up the next "Not So Common Courtesy @ Work" – maybe you will see yourself in it, Speaker-Phone-Abuser!" Or, better yet,

let the person know that their behavior is distracting to you and could they please not use speaker phone any longer? Much better approach.

10. And finally, an ingenious way to use this book: change someone's life by being courteous. You might be the event that puts a smile into someone's heart.

I know we can get back to a place where we really do think about others. I definitely see examples of beautiful Common Courtesy on our planet. Every time I do, I smile and my heart grows. It does. I would love to be smiling all day because I've seen so many examples of courtesy, respect, goodness and care for others, wouldn't you? Pass this dying knowledge along…or deal with the consequences (don't know what they are? Read the book again!).

Thank you for your time and attention, and I hope you have a very nice day!

(See how nice that sounded…go say that to some stranger on the street and make his or her day!)

Sometimes when we are generous in small, barely detectable ways it can change someone else's life forever.

Margaret Cho

Pass-it-Along-Pages

These pages are to rip right out of the book (sorry no perforations) and give to people you deem worthy of receiving them. Have fun! AND – I've left you some blank pages to make up your own messages. I know, I am living the courteous dream – go me!

Pass-it-Along-Pages

Tip of the Day - Read:

Not So Common Courtesy
By Mitzi Taylor

See if you can find yourself in there!

www.notsocommoncourtesy.com

Tip of the Day - Read:

Not So Common Courtesy
By Mitzi Taylor

See if you can find yourself in there!

www.notsocommoncourtesy.com

Pass-it-Along-Pages

Hey!

This book's for you!

www.notsocommoncourtesy.com

Hey!

This book's for you!

www.notsocommoncourtesy.com

I just thought I would let you know, that I appreciate your Courtesy. You are an example and inspiration to the world around you!

THANK YOU!

www.notsocommoncourtesy.com

I just thought I would let you know, that I appreciate your Courtesy. You are an example and inspiration to the world around you!

THANK YOU!

www.notsocommoncourtesy.com

Pass-it-Along-Pages

Pass-it-Along-Pages

Thank you for thanking me!

(I always feel so good when I get a "thank you" but am never sure how to do a "thank you for thanking me" thing. So here you go!)

www.notsocommoncourtesy.com

Thank you for thanking me!

(I always feel so good when I get a "thank you" but am never sure how to do a "thank you for thanking me" thing. So here you go!)

www.notsocommoncourtesy.com

Pass-it-Along-Pages

I am sure you are a very nice person, but you are hiding that fact really well. Next time, please hold the door for the person that is walking right behind you carrying three grocery bags and a baby. They will appreciate it more than you know.

Thank you in advance.

www.notsocommoncourtesy.com

I am sure you are a very nice person, but you are hiding that fact really well. Next time, please hold the door for the person that is walking right behind you carrying three grocery bags and a baby. They will appreciate it more than you know.

Thank you in advance.

www.notsocommoncourtesy.com

*Do one kind, unselfish thing today.
And smile.*

www.notsocommoncourtesy.com

Pass-it-Along-Pages

*Do one kind, unselfish thing today.
And smile.*

www.notsocommoncourtesy.com

Pass-it-Along-Pages – Make up Your Own

Pass-it-Along-Pages – Make up Your Own

Pass-it-Along-Pages – Make up Your Own

Resources:

Add more before passing this on. Also, email me so I can add them to the website and/or to future books!

Websites worth your time:

- www.payitforwardfoundation.org
  To educate and inspire students to realize that they can change the world, and provide them with opportunities to do so.

- www.helpothers.org
  "Kindness is contagious. Welcome to a portal dedicated to small acts of kindness".

- www.actsofkindness.org

  The Random Acts of Kindness™ Foundation inspires people to practice kindness and to "pass it on" to others.

More Resources:

Photo by Eidetic Imaging

Once upon a time, there was a little girl named Mitzi. She was born. She grew up. She wanted to live in a beautiful world where everyone treated each other with kindness and respect. She figured the best way to accomplish this was to get a lot of work experience so she could relate to every unique individual (retail, banking, manufacturing, family owned business), buy a business that helped businesses treat people with kindness and respect (Owner, Not So Basic Training) and write about ways we can all improve to make the world a better place. Ta-da! She did it all! I tell ya, what a great tale ☺

Ok, if you need more detail here you go:
- Bachelor's Degree from Western Michigan University (Organizational Communications/Marketing)
- Worked in many industries looking for that dream job
- Started at Not So Basic Training in 2000; Bought Not So Basic Training in 2003
- Wrote Not So Common Courtesy in 2008
- Lives in Muskegon with her dog - 65lbs-of-Need-Lucy
- Dream: Leave the world better than I found it

Made in the USA
Charleston, SC
12 October 2010